Weapon of Mass Destruction "Breathe Again"

Tyeshia M. Thomas

Copyright © 2018 Tyeshia M. Thomas
All rights reserved.
Published by A.T. Destiny Awaits Group LLC
Cover designed by Chassitie Adams
ISBN-13: 978-1-7320181-1-2
All rights reserved. No part of this publication may be reproduced, stored in retrieval system, or transmitted in any form or by any means-electronic, mechanical, photocopy, recording or otherwise without written permission from the author. Email contact: atdestinyawaitsgroup@gmail.com

All Scripture taken from King James Version (KJV) Public Domain unless otherwise stated.

Scripture quotations marked (GNT) are from the Good News Translation in Today's English Version- Second Edition Copyright © 1992 by American Bible Society. Used by Permission.

New International Version (NIV) Holy Bible, New International Version®, NIV® Copyright ©1973, 1978, 1984, 2011 by Biblica, Inc.® Used by permission. All rights reserved worldwide.

"Scripture quotations marked Amplified Bible are taken from Amplified Bible, Classic Edition (AMPC) Copyright © 1954, 1958, 1962, 1964, 1965, 1987 by The Lockman Foundation Used by permission.www.Lockman.org"

Scripture taken from The Voice™. Copyright © 2008 by Ecclesia Bible Society. Used by permission. All rights reserved.

Scripture is taken from GOD'S WORD®, © 1995 God's Word to the Nations. Used by permission of Baker Publishing Group.

Scripture quotations marked NLT are taken from the *Holy Bible*, New Living Translation, copyright © 1996, 2004, 2015 by Tyndale House Foundation. Used by permission of Tyndale House Publishers, Inc., Carol Stream, Illinois 60188. All rights reserved.

"Scripture taken from *The Message*. Copyright © 1993, 1994, 1995, 1996, 2000, 2001, 2002. Used by permission of NavPress Publishing Group."
The Living Bible copyright © 1971 by Tyndale House Foundation. Used by permission of Tyndale House Publishers Inc., Carol Stream, Illinois 60188. All rights reserved. The Living Bible, TLB, and the The Living Bible logo are registered trademarks of Tyndale House Publishers.

Weapon of Mass Destruction
"Breathe Again"

I GIFT THIS BOOK TO

_____

THIS _____ DAY OF _____, _____.

MAY GOD BLESS AND COMFORT YOU, AS YOU READ EACH PAGE IN JESUS NAME.

WITH LOVE,

_____

AMEN.

DEDICATION

I dedicate this devotional to you and all those who remained steadfast and unmovable, in times of being hurt, broken and rejected. To every weapon of mass destruction that is, has been and will be broken, before the Lord. I pray blessings and favor over you. Thank you for not wavering, when you could have because your laboring is not in vain.
Mama Mary "Ease" Kouaoh & Mama Sheila Lawrence "Breathe Again"

Weapon of Mass Destruction, it is time to "Breathe Again!"

TABLE OF CONTENTS

My Pity Party Interrupted

"THE EXPERIENCE"

Day One	Hang in there
Day Two	Don't stop waiting
Day Three	Don't let this stop you
Day Four	You will be revived
Day Five	You're surrounded by grace
Day Six	Looking beyond the "But"
Day Seven	God is fixing it!
Day Eight	Today is a New day!
Day Nine	Just Stay Calm
Day Ten	The Appointed Time
Day Eleven	Brethren Know that you're loved
Day Twelve	Today is a day of letting go
Day Thirteen	Today is a day of no regrets
Day Fourteen	Trust God with it
Day Fifteen	God Only
Day Sixteen	You're always on His mind
Day Seventeen	It was Good for me to be afflicted
Day Eighteen	He's our way out
Day Nineteen	From the Standpoint of Faith
Day Twenty	He Knew

Day Twenty-One	A Day of Listening
Day Twenty-Two	Yet, He still chose you
Day Twenty-Three	Today is our day of worship
Day Twenty-Four	God will replenish you
Day Twenty-Five	A day of Tremendous Things
Day Twenty-Six	Don't give up
Day Twenty-Seven	Welcome to your harvest season
Day Twenty-Eight	Just sit right here
Day Twenty-Nine	Today is your day to Shout
Day Thirty	Reaffirming in Christ
Day Thirty-One	Reaffirming Strength in God
Day Thirty-Two	Living past your reality
Day Thirty-Three	Reflecting on God
Day Thirty-Four	Reclaiming Structure
Day Thirty-Five	Reaffirming my verbiage
Day Thirty-Six	Reevaluating your circle
Day Thirty-Seven	Reaffirming your choice
Day Thirty-Eight	Reaffirming it had a purpose
Day Thirty-Nine	Reaffirming the King in my life
Day Forty	Everything Starts and Ends with

GOD

Weapon of Mass Destruction
"Breathe Again"

ACKNOWLEDGMENTS

To God, my Father: Thank you for sustaining me through every trial, tribulation, and persecution. Thank you for filling my life with more of you and less of myself. Thank you for leading me into deep waters and keeping me anchored in you, every step of the way. I love you more than the many words in the human vocabulary.

To my husband: Anthony J. Thomas, thank you for your sacrifice because I know it is hard to share me with a world of unknowns. You are the best husband, for me! I love and appreciate you! Thank you for laughter when I'm sad and mad. Thank you for expressing the hard truth, when I need to hear it (though I don't always welcome it).

To my children, God-children and grandchildren: Thank you for all you do! You are my reasons for many things. I thank God for blessing me with each of you! I love you, all very much!

To my powerful spiritual influences in this season: Apostle Paul Horn, Reverend Tracey Horn, Reverend James Williams, Bishop Loretta Smith- Johnson, Pastor Alexis Johnson (General), Overseer Joel Nicholas Parrish, and Dr. Robin Eubanks, Thank you all for pouring into my life and stretching me, as the Lord allows. I love you, all!

To my inner circle: Words will never be able to express how much I appreciate each of you. Thank you for being my true friends. Thank you for giving it to me straight. Thank you for being present in my darkest hours. Thank you for listening, fussing, encouraging, reminding and most importantly praying for me and with me. I'm grateful to God for you all. You all exemplify Proverbs 27:6 well! I love you, all!

To my graphic designer: Chassitie Adams, I love and appreciate you! Thank you for listening to my indecisiveness and helping me fulfill the vision that God has placed in me.

To my Weapon of Mass Destruction family: I love you all! I appreciate your support, prayers, emails, and text messages. It means more than you know. Thank you!

Weapon of Mass Destruction
"Breathe Again"

Introduction
My Pity Party Interrupted

Weapon of destruction you're not alone because I can relate. You may be like I was asking yourself how did I get here? How could I have allowed myself to hold my breath for so long? How could I walk around just existing and not living the life I was so blessed to live?

You may be saying to yourself, "I feel like I am stuck in between my yesterday and today. I feel like if I could just Breathe again maybe my life would take a turn for the better. I am surrounded by so many people, but drowning in loneliness. I hear the noise around me, but my life has no sound. My vibrancy left me, and my self-esteem seems too low. I often wonder where did, I lay it and why did it have to go.

Where did I misplace my self-esteem and identity this time? "Was it during my last intimate encounter, or is it with that best friend that betrayed me yet again. Maybe it is in my last mistake, that caused me all that shame or are my children walking around with it and do they really know their name? Have my decisions and choices impacted my children to the point of no return?"

Then suddenly my pity party was interrupted by a voice on the inside saying, "If you don't mind I would like to interrupt right here and make a life altering declaration over your life. I decree and declare that you shall live and not die."

Weapon of Mass Destruction I command you to breathe again. I command your memory to recall the last time God's love touched you tangibly. Maybe it was the last cashier that gave you an extraordinary pleasant greeting or the smile of some stranger. Maybe it was a long-lost friend through a phone call just calling to check on you.

Weapon of Mass Destruction life can get challenging and circumstances can seem unbearable sometimes, but I encourage you to breathe again. Breathe like you did before this last thing happened. Breathe like you did before you experienced this loss. Breathe again like you did before the last encounter with betrayal. It's imperative for you to breathe again. You are treasured by God and He loves you more than you feel beyond what you can imagine. He just needs you to be open and let Him in. Allow Him to go deeper.

Over the next forty days I pray that God will cause you to experience great revival. I pray that refreshing will hit your life. I pray that He will intervene on your behalf. I pray that the diagnosis lines up with the will of our Chief Physician in Heaven according to Isaiah 53:5. I pray that Your heart will be mended for God is near to the broken hearted according to Psalm 34:18.

Weapon of Mass Destruction
"Breathe Again"

Breathe again. Inhale and exhale. That's life worth living. Inhale and exhale that's a miracle. Inhale and exhale you're going to make it through this. Inhale Peace and exhale anxiety. Inhale trust in God and exhale self- reliance. Inhale the love of God and exhale the hate of every enemy.

Weapon of Mass Destruction are you ready for this type of change? Let the Potter make you anew by committing to spend time in His word daily.
Do you commit to this? If so, turn the page and let the process begin

GOD Speaks

2 Corinthians 4:16-18 states, "So we have no reason to despair. Despite the fact that our outer humanity is falling apart and decaying, our inner humanity is breathing in new life every day. [17] You see, the short-lived pains of this life are creating for us an eternal glory that does not compare to anything we know here. [18] So we do not set our sights on the things we can see with our eyes. All of that is fleeting; it will eventually fade away. Instead, we focus on the things we cannot see, which live on and on." (VOICE)

Weapon of Mass Destruction
"Breathe Again"

"THE EXPERIENCE"

Weapon of Mass Destruction have you ever experienced feelings of true suffocation? What I mean is have you ever been in a place where it seemed you was really suffocating? Maybe you have been in a position where you felt that you were too closed in and could not get any relief?

Weapon of Mass Destruction, I remember a time when I experienced feelings of true life suffocation. I was at a place in my life where it seemed like I was really suffocating. I was in a position in life where I felt I was too closed in to breathe and could not find any outside relief.

I'm not talking about just losing my breath for a moment. I'm talking about being so closed in that it felt like if I did not catch my breath; I was not going to make it. I was at a point in my life where nothing seemed like it was coming together. There were days I felt like I was having an asthma attack without having asthma. I remember being in rooms filled with people and inwardly wishing someone could breathe for me.

Weapon of Mass Destruction there are things that happen in our lives, and they have the potential to leave us feeling trapped in between our yesterday's troubles and our tomorrow's problems. There are situations that will have us questioning who God created us to be and who people try to make us out to be. There are instances in life, where we can fall into error, by living accepted by people, but rejected by God and absent from his anointing. Sometimes during this Christian journey, we find out how easy it is to fall into the role of just looking the part, as opposed to being the part that God created us to be.

Weapon of Mass Destruction if this is you I command you to breathe again or maybe you are the one that has felt like you have been sucker punched by life and got the wind knocked out of you. That incident has left you feeling some type of way, and since that day it has seemed like the air has been slowly but surely seeping out your life.

Weapon of Mass Destruction place your right hand on your head, left hand on stomach, gently push, and recite the following five commands out loud; Self, I command you to be free. I command you to let go of yesterday's failures and breathe again. I command every anxiety to loose you and let you go. I command fear to get out, immediately. I command spiritual leeches to let you go now in Jesus name.

Now, Weapon of Mass Destruction, Breathe Again. 2 Timothy 1:7 promises, God has not given you the spirit of fear, but He gives love, power, and a sound mind.

Weapon of Mass Destruction it is time for you to stop merely existing and breathe again. Yes, the thief comes to steal, kill and destroy but Jesus promised He

Weapon of Mass Destruction
"Breathe Again"

came so that we may have life and have it more abundantly.

    Weapon of Mass Destruction suffocation in a supernatural sense can cause you to feel trapped and oppressed. It can make you feel that your airway is being blocked and can prevent the access of air from getting to the blood through the lungs.

    In a natural sense, to breathe is take in air, oxygen into your lungs and expel it. Breathing is important because our cells constantly need a new supply of oxygen to produce energy. A lack of oxygen causes cells and organs in our body began to get damaged. Inhaling supplies the oxygen needed, that is vital for our physical survival, and your exhale rids the body of the carbon dioxide, waste products, and toxins. In the supernatural sense, breathing can be defined as living a more abundant life by trusting God with every fiber of your being.

    Weapon of Mass Destruction Breathe Again. God has it all under control. I need you to inhale faith and exhale doubt. I need you to inhale fresh fire and exhale exhaustion. I need you to inhale the newness in God and exhale the old. Breathe again. You're going to get through this Breathe Again. Breathe in the bread of life and exhale every contamination. Weapon of Mass Destruction it is imperative that you Breathe Again. It's ok to Breathe Again! I need you to inhale and exhale.

I need you to live as if it never happened. I need you to live like you did before the betrayal happened. I need you to live like people never let you down. I need you to live like the disappointment never came. I need you to live. The Kingdom of God has need of you! We need you to breathe again.

Weapon of Mass Destruction, you shall live and not die from this blow.

Weapon of Mass Destruction God has granted us access to His throne. Our fullness of joy resides in His presence. It's imperative Weapon of Mass Destruction that you Breathe again! You're more than enough! You're more than a conqueror! You're an overcomer! Weapon of Mass Destruction it's time for you to Breathe Again! Let's enter in……

Father God in the name of Jesus, the name that is above every name, here we are longing to know how to breathe again. We come longing to get past where we are. Take us Lord in our time of prayer, study, worship, and meditation to the place that we've read about and have seen in our visions. Thank you in advance. Amen

GOD Speaks

Isaiah 43:18-19 states, "Remember ye not the former things, neither consider the things of old. Behold, I will do a new thing; now it shall spring forth; shall ye not know it? I will even make a way in the wilderness, and rivers in the desert." (KJV)

Day One
Hang in there

"May we never tire of doing what is good and right before our Lord because in His season we shall bring in a great harvest if we can just persist."
(Galatians 6:9, VOICE)

Good Morning Weapon of Mass Destruction,

 I'm truly excited to be able to begin this journey of recovery with you. I thank God for His many translations of the Bible that causes us to get a better understanding of His word. I have grown to love the King James Version of this scripture but as I begin to explore the arrangements of the words in other translations I was very intrigued and most encouraged from this translation.

 There are many things that happen in life and ministry that sometimes throws you for a loop. We are presented with challenges, daily. Sometimes, they seem a little too hard to face. Challenges that cause us to want to reevaluate who we are and where we are.

 Weapon of Mass Destruction, I encourage you this morning to hang in there and keep doing what's right. I'm reminded of Deuteronomy 30:15 (Voice) "Look, I've given you *two* choices today: you can have life with all the good things it brings, or death and all the bad things it brings." I encourage you today to choose life. No matter what is going on in your life to keep on going and don't give up. You're on the edge of your breakthrough. I know it's hard right now, but God **cannot** lie. His word is true and shall stand. Your harvest shall be great! Keep doing what's right, Breathe and hang in there.

Father God in the name of Jesus. I pray for a renewal of strength, right now over myself and every other person reading this book, and that will read this book. Lord God, I pray for perseverance to come forth in our lives now. Lord, please continue to sustain us in ways that are far greater than our imaginations. We love, and need you in our lives in Jesus name we pray. Amen

Day Two
Don't stop waiting

"But they that wait upon the Lord shall renew their strength. They shall mount up with wings like eagles; they shall run and not be weary; they shall walk and not faint."
(Isaiah 40:31, TLB)

Good Morning Weapon of Mass Destruction,

    I hope you slept well on last night and awakened this morning with an "any moment now" expectation. I am expecting with you at any moment now your situation is taking a turn for the better. It's like rushing to the airport to pick someone up only to find out when you get there that the plane has been delayed because of bad weather and unsafe landing conditions. So now you're there waiting with an indefinite wait time. You know it's coming but just don't know exactly when the weather is going to permit the plane to land safely. At that point, you can choose to stay there and wait or leave the airport and risk the chance of not being there when the plane lands.

    Weapon of Mass Destruction I encourage you to wait on God. As hard as it may seem and as urgent that your situation appears God is right there working it out for your good. Your greater and better is coming any moment now! God won't fail you. Your release is going to get to you any moment now. It's worth the wait. God knows what your miracle needs to survive once it gets to you. Weapon of Mass Destruction Breathe and don't stop waiting.

Father God in the name of Jesus, I pray that You would increase Godly patience within me and every vessel that will read this book. I pray that we will not be allowed to give up before the appointed time of our breakthrough. Lord grant us peace during the wait and strength to make it to our promise. Thank you, Father. Amen

Day Three
Don't let this stop you

"Many hardships *and* perplexing circumstances confront the righteous, But the LORD rescues him from them all."
(Psalm 34:19, AMP)

Good Morning Weapon of Mass Destruction,

I pray that you are daily being encouraged, and at peace as you sleep. Today, I want you to focus on the Truth that God is coming to your rescue. I was reading 2 Samuel 22 on last night, and as I read line by line, I felt myself being strengthened. I felt my Rescuer near. Though I was suffering, yet another hardship God came to see about my wellbeing.

Weapon of Mass Destruction, God knows best. He loves us too much to leave us lonely and helpless. In fact, His word teaches us today that we as His righteous children in Jesus Christ are confronted by many hardships and circumstances, but it doesn't stop there. It gives a "But!" Hallelujah, we can look at the three-letter word "but" to be an indicator that what is after the "but" is better than what was before. The Lord's rescue is much better than any hardship that we are currently facing, and any hardship, circumstance and challenge that we will every face.

Weapon of Mass Destruction
"Breathe Again"

    Weapon of Mass Destruction that is more than enough to shout unto God, "I need You Jesus; to come to my rescue."

    I believe if you shouted that where you are that God has responded already to your praise. Hallelujah!

    Father God in the name of Jesus, Thank You for inhabiting my praise and the praises of every person reading this book. Lord God, I pray that our praise made the dam that's been standing between us and our many blessings to break. I call the blessings of God forth in our lives. Lord give us an indication today that it is You that is coming to our rescue in Jesus name. Amen

Day Four
You will be revived

> "He said to me, "Mortal man, can these bones come back to life?" I replied, "Sovereign LORD, only you can answer that!"
> (Ezekiel 37:3, GNT)

Good Morning Weapon of Mass Destruction,

    I must say that I'm shouting for the 4th day of our Journey Thank You Lord. I am reminded of the tribe of Judah. The 4th child the one lineage chosen for our Lord and Savior Jesus to come through. Today gives me hope that this is the day God will turn it around to work in our favor.

    Weapon of Mass Destruction I hope you're inhaling the gift of life each day and exhaling every ounce of worry, doubt, stress, discouragement, and hopelessness.

    I love our lesson today, and it brings me great joy. I believe this is one of my favorite chapters in the book of Ezekiel. This verse gave me hope during the enemy trying to make me think I was hopeless.

    Our lesson began with the words mortal man, and it reminded me of how limited we are without God. How limited our ability is apart from The Word. God asks a question can these bones come back to life? In other words, can

Weapon of Mass Destruction
"Breathe Again"

what that has been considered dead, useless, unfruitful, ineffective of no purpose come back to life? Can it be fruitful again, effective and bring God glory? I love the response, "Sovereign Lord, only You can answer that!" Hallelujah. I believe the writer was saying, "God I acknowledge you can do whatever it is You want to do and God, I know You to be Able."

Weapon of Mass Destruction, I encourage you to begin to tell God who He is to you, not what you need Him to do today, but who You acknowledge Him to be to you. Do you consider Him a Big God or minute? Only you can answer that, but I assure you God can make every dead thing in our lives live again.

Weapon of Mass Destruction, Breathe again. Inhale Faith that God Can and exhale what you are facing right now because it is the right size for God to do what is impossible with men.

Father God in the name of Jesus, I pray that you will increase my faith and the faith of every person that will read this book with each day that passes, according to Your word that faith cometh by hearing and hearing by the Word of God. I thank You in advance for the manifestations that our faith will produce and bring You, Father greater glory in Jesus name. Amen

Tyeshia M. Thomas

GOD Speaks

*Isaiah 53:5 (Voice) explains, "But he was hurt because of us; he suffered so.
Our wrongdoing wounded and crushed him.
He endured the breaking that made us whole.
The injuries he suffered became our healing."*

Weapon of Mass Destruction
"Breathe Again"

Day Five
You're surrounded by grace

"After you have suffered for a little while, the God of grace who has called you [to His everlasting presence] through Jesus the Anointed will restore you, support you, strengthen you, and ground you. For all power belongs to God, now and forever. Amen."
(1 Peter 5:10-11, The Voice)

Good Morning Weapon of Mass Destruction,

    Welcome to our new day of grace! A day filled with fresh new mercies ready and waiting for us to need of them. I'm a little giddy this morning because our passage of scripture today promises we will be restored. That means we will be reinstated to our right place. Our joy will be reinstated. The privileges we once enjoyed will be reinstated. It's kind of like having too many speeding tickets and losing our license to operate a vehicle for a period.

    During my own personal process, I remember thanking God for allowing me to have still been alive on day five. As time progressed and the situation I was in seemed like it was getting worse, without evidence of improvement; the harder it seemed for me, to trust God.

    Weapon of Mass Destruction, for both our sakes it is imperative for me to be honest. I'm learning that some of the processes that God allows us to go through in life can leave us feeling like we suffered a big loss of many privileges. Sometimes, it is from our disobedience while other times, it is just our vehicle to getting to the next realm of His glory, favor and another level of faith.

For instance, bills piling up and you don't have the money to pay them. There's no one to call. All options exhausted and only one thing to do, trust God. It is like receiving a bad doctor report that doesn't line up with the healing described in Isaiah 53:5 and no one can help BUT God.

So, Weapon of Mass Destruction if you are feeling like I was feeling then I encourage you to thank God for still being alive on day five.

Weapon of Mass Destruction, at times like this, be encouraged because you are surrounded by grace, Isaiah 53:5. Five is the number of grace, three represents the Blessed Trinity, and then five again makes it complete. We are engulfed by grace in the blessed Trinity.

Weapon of Mass Destruction, thank God for grace. God is the only one I know who can take our many messes and turn every one of them into a message. He's the only one I know that can make hopeless situations hopeful. The only one I know that can make a negative a positive.

Weapon of Mass Destruction
"Breathe Again"

Weapon of Mass Destruction God is the one that chose the foolish things of the world to shame the wise; God chose the weak things of the world to shame the strong. (1 Corinthians 1:27) He's the only one that I know that allows the race not to be given to the swift, nor the battle to the strong, neither yet bread to the wise, nor yet riches to men of understanding, nor yet favour to men of skill; but He is the One that allows time and chance to happen to them all. (Ecclesiastes 9:11, KJV)

Weapon of Mass Destruction BREATHE AGAIN. BREATHE IN GRACE. Have confidence in Romans 8:38-39 which states, "For I am persuaded, that neither death, nor life, nor angels, nor principalities, nor powers, nor things present, nor things to come, Nor height, nor depth, nor any other creature, shall be able to separate us from the love of God, which is in Christ Jesus our Lord."

Father God in the name of Jesus thank You for knowing all things and surrounding us with your grace. Thank You for Your love and compassion. Thank You for being incomparable and mighty. Thank You for being genuine and true. You are Amazing, and your presence is like no other. Amen

Tyeshia M. Thomas

Day Six
Looking beyond the "But"

"But the God of all grace, who hath called us unto his eternal glory by Christ Jesus, after that ye have suffered a while, make you perfect, stablish, strengthen, settle you. To him be glory and dominion for ever and ever. Amen."
(1 Peter 5:10-11, KJV)

Good Morning Weapon of Mass Destruction,

    Our scripture passage on yesterday was good. After spending so much time explaining the restoration of it, there wasn't enough time to address the message in its entirety. Today, we will look at it in the King James Version translation.

    The King James version begins with "but" and as I previously mentioned I love the But because it assures me that everything before the but is irrelevant. "But" as a conjunction has several definitions and the one that stood out most was this one; but means to introduce something contrasting with what has already been mentioned. A synonym of the word but is Nonetheless.

    Our text begins with But "The" God not "A" God, but "The" God and it doesn't stop there. It gets better by saying of All grace. Grace is unmerited and undeserved favor. I don't know about you, but that makes me want to shout for joy because in the midst of me sometimes feeling like I'm not enough and I'm not worthy; this scripture text reminds me that I serve the God of All grace. Hallelujah.

Weapon of Mass Destruction this verse should serve as a reminder to us that we are called, but not just by anyone. We are called by the Eternal, Everlasting God who grants us unmerited and undeserved favor. The God that doesn't lie. The God that makes promises and keeps them and not because we're deserving of them.

I'll stop here today and remind you that your laboring is not in vain. This too shall pass! God shall make you perfect, establish you, strengthen you and settle you. God is freeing us from fault. He is making us stable. He is making us stronger and securing us, permanently. God is our guarantee, and He is more than enough!

Weapon of Mass Destruction, God made us a promise! I encourage you to be filled with a Nonetheless & But God in your spirit as you inhale the favor of God and exhale every frustrating thought in the name of Jesus.

LOOK BEYOND THE BUT AND BREATHE AGAIN!

Father God in the name of Jesus look upon me, the people that have read this book, and the people that will read it. Lord, fill us with the nonetheless that Jesus had in the garden of Gethsemane. Daddy, cause us to be strengthened to the point that we can endure, as Jesus endured. Heavenly Father, cause our reward of victory over the enemy to become more evident. Open our eyes to see the power that we have over the enemy that Jesus promised in Luke 10:19, in Jesus name I pray. Amen

Weapon of Mass Destruction
"Breathe Again"

Day Seven
God is fixing it!

"He sent His word, and healed them, and delivered them from their destructions."
(Psalm 107:20, KJV)

Good Morning Weapon of Mass Destruction,

    I thank God for the simplicity of your life today. I thank Him for waking you up this morning. You are truly an answer to prayer. You are fearfully and wonderfully made by God. Today's scripture lesson has truly blessed my life. I thank God for our day of completion.

    Our scripture text began with He sent His word. The He isn't referring to just any He, it is talking about the Maker and Creator of Heaven, Earth, the sea and all that is within them. It's talking about the ONE that spoke everything into existence. The atmosphere conforms to what He speaks. It is talking about the ONE that promised us that His word would not return unto Him void.

    Weapon of Mass Destruction this gave me great hope because it assured me that even if I caused myself to get in the shape I'm in God still has the power to deliver me. Romans 2:11 states, "For there is no respect of persons with God." (KJV) Just like He did it for King David, He will do it for you and me! Hallelujah! Hold on because there is still hope! God is fixing it! God is coming to our rescue! He will change our situation just in the nick of time. He sent His word, and His word is powerful! It is precise! It is the Truth!

Weapon of Mass Destruction, God is fixing it!

Father in the name of Jesus, thank you for fixing it. I thank You for completion in all things. Father, I pray for an everlasting change in my life and the lives of the people that will read this book. Father God send the word that everything in our lives causing us harm will be eternally changed, never to return to this state in Jesus name. Amen

Day Eight
Today is a New day!

"In the beginning was the Word, and the Word was with God and the Word was God."
(St John 1:1, KJV)

Good Morning Weapon of Mass Destruction,

Welcome to our day of new beginnings. I thank God for granting you the new. We are being given rest to regroup and time to gather our thoughts. Today, I believe we will witness the manifestation of the evidence of being internally refilled and revived by God from the inside out.

Weapon of Mass Destruction, Expect it Today!

Our passage of scripture takes us back to the beginning. It's reminding us to think about the beginning. In the beginning, everything was already provided for Adam and Eve. Everything! They had no worries because God had already prepared it for them. Be encouraged today because Jesus is the Word and He has fulfilled the requirements to place us back in right standing with God. The beginning blessings. I call forth the beginning blessings and ask God to direct them to us in Jesus name.

This is our day of new beginnings the 8th day! Hallelujah and because it is a new beginning I have to stop here and make sure you have accepted the gift God has given you. Have you accepted Jesus Christ as Lord and Savior of Your life? If you haven't then these blessings will be held up from getting to you until you make the decision to accept God's gift of salvation that only comes through Jesus the Christ.

Romans 10:9 states, That if thou shalt confess with thy mouth the Lord Jesus, and shalt believe in thine heart that God hath raised him from the dead, thou shalt be saved. (KJV)

It is that easy! I know that it sounds unbelievable, but it is not. Here is a prayer that will help get the process started.

Lord God, I am a sinner, and I need to be saved. Please forgive me for all of my sins and teach me how to live for you. I believe your son, Jesus died for me. I believe he rose for me. Lord, Jesus come into my life and be my Lord and Savior. Thank you for saving me. Amen

Weapon of Mass Destruction, if you prayed this prayer and accepted your gift. I would love to hear from you. Please feel free to leave me a message under the contact me section of our website www.atdestinyawaits.com

Day Nine
Just Stay Calm

"But Moses told the people, "Don't be afraid. Just stand still and watch the Lord rescue you today. The Egyptians you see today will never be seen again. The Lord himself will fight for you. Just stay calm."
(Exodus 14:13-14, NLT)

Good Morning Weapon of Mass Destruction,

I thank God for divine completeness. Not only are we in a new beginning in the natural but our spiritual being has received a divine completeness from God. One of the many things I love about God is His ability to fight for us. His ability to come to our rescue and be right on time.

Weapon of Mass Destruction, I encourage you today to just stay calm. It doesn't matter what comes up against you. I need you just to stay calm. The Lord, our God, is coming to your rescue.

Although, the children of Israel escaped from Egypt; there was still another battle to be fought, and this battle would be different.

Weapon of Mass Destruction the battle you are facing right now is different because God is going to fight for you. Just stay calm, don't be afraid and watch God do what you can't do for yourself.

The children of Israel stood at the red sea with the enemy on their trail. They had nowhere else to go. God caused the sea to open up, and they experienced God's power in a way that was new. God rescued them from the enemy, and he is going to do the same for you. Just Stay Calm.

Father God, Our rescuer, in the name of Jesus, we come presenting ourselves unto you. We come casting all our worries on you. Lord, it seems like there is no way out of this, but we trust you. Lord, we need you to fight for us just like you did for the children of Israel. We need you to come to our rescue. Teach us how to remain calm in the midst of wanting to compromise what you promised us just to get a break. Lord God grant us a breath of fresh air. We believe what you said. We decree and declare that we will stand still and watch you rescue us. Thank you for providing us with the courage to wait, in Jesus name. Amen

Day Ten
The Appointed Time

"This is God's Word on the subject: "As soon as Babylon's seventy years are up and not a day before, I'll show up and take care of you as I promised and bring you back home. I know what I'm doing. I have it all planned out—plans to take care of you, not abandon you, plans to give you the future you hope for." (Jeremiah 29:11, MSG)

Good Morning Weapon of Mass Destruction,

I awakened this morning so refreshed, and filled with an unspeakable kind of joy. Nothing spectacular has really happened besides I'm awake and well. I looked over at my husband, and he was breathing. I'm just so excited to see what God has for me today, and I hope you are too.

Our scripture lesson today gives hope. It begins with God's word on the subject. What is God's word on your subject? It is important to know what God says about our situations. We must understand that God has appointed a time for us to come out.

Weapon of Mass Destruction, God has an appointed time to take care of what is causing you to worry. He has an expiration date for it to be complete and your situation will respond to God's time table. Deliverance will come forth in

God's timing. The manifestation of healings will come forth in God's timing.

    All Knowing, Almighty God, in Heaven, We come to You saying, "Thank you for our appointed time." Lord, though we do not see our end from the beginning, we know that you are present in them both. Lord, there are times when your timing seems so far away. At those times, Father, we ask that the Holy Spirit within us bring back to our remembrance every promise that will comfort us at that moment. Lord God, teach us how to wait patiently on you alone. Teach us how to have our expectations in you no matter what. Lord grant us insight that will cause us to gain a deeper appreciation for our appointed time. Lord, we love you and thank you for endowing us with your everlasting love in Jesus name we pray. Amen

Day Eleven
Brethren Know that you're loved

"For God expressed His love for the world in this way: He gave His only Son so that whoever believes in Him will not face everlasting destruction, but will have everlasting life."
(John 3:16, VOICE)

Good Morning Weapon of Mass Destruction,

I'm thinking of you and praying to the God we serve. I pray that your today will better than your yesterday. I thank God for being with you in your time of need and despair. When I think of His love for us, it amazes me every time. I encourage you this morning to think about the worst thing you've done. Now think on the fact that God knows about it and still loves you. That alone makes me say Wow because I know the many times I've been guilty.

Weapon of Mass Destruction, today I want you to take the time to let the following word sink in: For God so loved you that He gave His only begotten Son Jesus to die on the cross for you, and be raised from the dead for you to have everlasting spiritual life available to you. Hallelujah!

"But *think about this:* while we were wasting our lives in sin, God revealed His powerful love to us *in a tangible display*—the Anointed One died for us." (Romans 5:8, The Voice)

    Heavenly Father we come praising you and thanking you for your incomparable love. Lord, we can't wrap our minds around the fullness of your love because it is so much. Lord, we honor you for being Lord over our lives. We love you and everything about you. Thank you for being right here with us in Jesus name we pray. Amen

Weapon of Mass Destruction
"Breathe Again"

Day Twelve
Today is a day of letting go

Focused on the Goal

"I'm not saying that I have this all together, that I have it made. But I am well on my way, reaching out for Christ, who has so wondrously reached out for me. Friends, don't get me wrong: By no means do I count myself an expert in all of this, but I've got my eye on the goal, where God is beckoning us onward — to Jesus. I'm off and running, and I'm not turning back." (Philippians 3:12-14, MSG)

Good Morning Weapon of Mass Destruction,

    I am so excited about our day of letting go. Let go, what we think it should be. Let go, how we thought we should have been treated. Let go of how far ahead we thought we should be. Today is the day to let go of yesterday and embrace the now. Let go the pain of yesterday. You may be asking, "I want to let go, but how do I, when it hurts so bad?" Confess it to God see, and seek His will, for your now.

    Our scripture text encourages us to keep our eye on the goal. What is your main goal? Our main goal should be fulfilling all God assigned us to fulfill. This may be hard sometimes, but it is possible. Ask God to help you and watch him do it.

Tyeshia M. Thomas

Heavenly Father, Thank you for today. Lord, it seems so hard to let go of things that have been a part of my life for so long. Lord what will I do with myself, if I let the "what if's" go? Lord, how do I let go the pain that came from what they did to me? Lord, how can I stop the images in my mind from getting the best of me? Lord, Help because I want to let it go.

Lord, I surrender my pain to you because I can't handle it. Lord, I surrender every memory to you because I need you to remove the pain from them. Lord, I surrender my will to you because I don't want to release them from how it made me feel. Lord, help me. I want to love again. I want to breathe again. I want to be able to trust again. I want to be able to live without self-restraints. Lord, please forgive me for holding on to these toxic things for so long. I desire to be free. Lord, I trust you, and I let go in you. Let your will be done, in Jesus name I pray. Amen

Day Thirteen
Today is a day of no regrets

"The steps of a [good and righteous] man are directed *and* established by the LORD, And He delights in his way [and blesses his path]."
(Psalm 37:23, MSG)

Good Morning Weapon of Mass Destruction,

I am so glad you are up and alert because today is our day of no regrets. Yesterday we let it go, and today we make a declaration that from this day forward we shall not live in regret. Our steps have been ordered by the Lord. We have been placed back in right standing with God, through the perfect sacrifice of Jesus, on the cross. No regrets. No should've, could've and didn't by mistake is worth carrying around with us. Especially, when the word of God assures us that our steps have been directed and established by the Lord. Yes, we are free will beings but do we actually have that much power to stop the Lord's will from being done in our lives. He can stop what He wants and allow what He wants.

Weapon of Mass Destruction, I believe there were some things in our lives that God didn't allow us to complete. I believe one of the reasons was it truly wasn't His will for us and It would've taken us off of our God intended path according to His predestined plan for us.

Weapon of Mass Destruction, BREATHE AGAIN AND DECLARE FROM THIS DAY FORWARD, I WILL LIVE MY LIFE FREE FROM REGRETS.

    Heavenly Father, Thank you for removing every regret that has held me bound. Thank you for setting me free by Your word. Lord thank you for ordering my steps and only allowing what you knew I could handle. Lord keep me in your will and don't let me stray away from your intended path for my life. I desire to breathe again in you. Thank you for being my God; the one that planned out my life before I accepted it as truth in Jesus name I pray. Amen

Weapon of Mass Destruction
"Breathe Again"

Day Fourteen
Trust God with it

"You haven't tried this before, but begin now. Ask, using my name, and you will receive, and your cup of joy will overflow." (John 16:24, TLB)

Good Morning Weapon of Mass Destruction,

    I encourage you this morning to trust God with it. You've tried everything else. Now trust God with it. You've racked your brain enough. Now trust God with it. It's just the right size for Him. It's bigger than you, and it was supposed to be because God wants you to trust Him with it. He knew there would come a time when you would get to this place. A time, when you would have tried to change what you are going through by every possible method and way you have known. Now, trust God with it. This is as good a day as any to trust God with it.

    Father God in the name of Jesus as me and my brothers and sisters in Christ go through our day trying with the best of our ability to trust You with it; fix it for us. Show us some evidence today that change is now and You are still in control. Lord, thank You for being able. Thank You for being willing to do exceeding abundantly more than we could ask or think according to Your Holy Word in Ephesians 3:20. We love you Lord God, and we're grateful that You are right here with us. Amen

Day Fifteen
God Only

"Come to Me, all who are weary and burdened, and I will give you rest. Put My yoke upon your shoulders — *it might appear heavy at first, but it is perfectly fitted to your curves.* Learn from Me, for I am gentle and humble of heart. *When you are yoked to Me,* your weary souls will find rest. For My yoke is easy, and My burden is light."
(Matthew 11:28-30, VOICE)

Good Morning Weapon of Mass Destruction,

    Today is a God only day. You may be asking, "What is a God only day?" Well, it's a day, when your reality loudly exclaims, "It's going to take God only, to change your circumstances!" God only transformation of your state of mind! It's going to take God only, to change the diagnosis! It's going to take God only, to pay off your immediate debt. It's going to take God only, to fix and heal your wounded heart! It's going to take God only, to help you forgive! Even in the midst of your reality screaming, God is saying, "I know it's a God only day, and I am able to supply all that you need." God is exclaiming, "Come to me my child, I can handle it for you! Talk to me, and tell me all about it. Hand me all your cares, and all your fears. I already know, it's too much for you to bare and too difficult for you to understand. That is why I am here. Trust Me! I just need you to give it to me. I'm a Gentleman. I will not make you give it to me, but

Weapon of Mass Destruction
"Breathe Again"

I will accept the responsibility of fixing it. At the point of your request, I'm here, I'm willing, I'm waiting on you, and I am listening. I love you more than you are able to imagine, and I can do in a moment, what would take you years to do yourself. Come to Me my child, and I will give you rest!"

Father God in the name of Jesus I come to you with petitions of my own within my heart, lifting up my brothers and sisters in you. Lord, touch us at our point of need. Heal us from feelings of desperation, and despair. Overshadow us with Your incomparable and unimaginable love. Thank You, Lord God for our lives, and for granting us the way to live, life more abundantly, through Your only begotten Son, Jesus Christ. Thank You, Lord. You are matchless in all of your ways in Jesus name I pray. Amen.

Day Sixteen
You're always on His mind

"Look here. I have *made you a part of Me,* written you on the palms of My hands. Your *city* walls are always on My mind, *always My concern."*
(Isaiah 49:16, VOICE)

Good Morning Weapon of Mass Destruction,

 Today is a day to remember. God personally made you apart of Himself. He is concerned with your well-being. It doesn't matter if man never acknowledges your importance. God is concerned about what concerns you.

 Weapon of Mass Destruction, we are all different on purpose. Our desires are different, but we were created to work in harmony with one another. For example; God may desire to display Himself to the world through you by loving people unconditionally. While yet, God desires to show Himself to the world through another by sacrificially giving financially.

 So you see, you enhance the body, and so do I. You are a vessel that God is concerned about, and so am I. The privilege is knowing God is concerned about us ALL.

 Our scripture today is intriguing to me. We are always on the mind of God, and I am grateful! Nothing and no one can change that!

Weapon of Mass Destruction
"Breathe Again"

God decides! Hallelujah! I hope you have a great day!

Weapon of Mass Destruction you can Breathe Again! God chose you to Breathe Again!

Heavenly Father, Thank You for every breath we are able to take. Thank you for reminding us that we are always on your mind. Thank you for the reminder that you are a concerned parent. Thank you for making us a part of you. We are forever grateful because we know without you, we would be eternal failures. Thank You for loving us more than we can imagine. Lord, thank You for extremely loving us in Jesus name we pray Amen

Day Seventeen
"It was Good for me to be afflicted"

It was good that I had to suffer
in order to learn your laws.
The teachings that come from your mouth are worth more to me
than thousands in gold or silver.
(Psalm 119:71-72, GW)

Good Morning Weapon of Mass Destruction,

I come to you this morning saying, "It was good for me to have been afflicted." It was good that I have lived life this far, well acquainted with long-suffering. It was good that I was persecuted, rejected, left, let down and counted out. In those times, I learned how to love God. I learned that God loves me. I learned that God loves to spend time with me. I learned how to cherish what He said more than what those around me said. I learned to believe His word. I learned how to be alone but know that I'm not alone.

So today Weapon of Mass Destruction I encourage you to think back and praise God because it was good for you to have been afflicted. Being afflicted caused you to be more compassionate to others that are experiencing affliction. Just think back of what you gained from the affliction and praise God.

Weapon of Mass Destruction
"Breathe Again"

Father God in Heaven, we take the time today to thank you for allowing us to have been afflicted.

Dear Lord, Thank you for having allowed us to go through affliction and come out, victoriously. Thank You for increasing our compassion towards others that are experiencing affliction. Thank You for increasing our faith. Thank You for causing us to be more sensitive to the needs of others. Hallelujah! Thank You for allowing us to know how to pray for those afflicted, and from an afflicted place. We honor You. We love You, and we are grateful that we were chosen to make it through in Jesus name we pray Amen

Day Eighteen
He's our way out

"No temptation [regardless of its source] has overtaken *or* enticed you that is not common to human experience [nor is any temptation unusual or beyond human resistance]; but God is faithful [to His word — He is compassionate and trustworthy], and He will not let you be tempted beyond your ability [to resist], but along with the temptation He [has in the past and is now and] will [always] provide the way out as well, so that you will be able to endure it [without yielding, and will overcome temptation with joy]."
(1 Corinthians 10:13, AMP)

Good Morning Weapon of Mass Destruction,

    I come to you this morning rejoicing because God is our way out. He has already provided us with everything we will need to get out. He knew we would be here. That's why he has already pre-arranged your escape. He is compassionate and trustworthy enough not to leave us in this shape. He knows you are stronger than you think. He knows you have what it takes. Your endurance is impeccable because of GOD.

    Weapon of Mass Destruction take a deep breath in and then exhale. There's no need to be discouraged. He is our way out. There isn't any need to get frustrated. He is our way out. No matter how much it feels like there is no way out, He is our way out. You may be asking, "How do you know?" My answer is because **He has no *favorites*!** Search out Romans 2:11 in as many translations that you can and see for yourself.

Heavenly Father in the name of Jesus thank you for being our way out of trouble, fear, depression, oppression and anything else that tries to hold us hostage. Thank you for being our way out of the grips of satan and every evil attachment. Thank you for filling us with your plans of escape. Holy Spirit, bring back to our remembrance the plans to prosper us that God has made available for us. Lord as we go back, fill us as we read the scripture text again. Touch us in our inner man and show us the way out of this in Jesus name we pray Amen

Day Nineteen
From the Standpoint of Faith

"For I consider [from the standpoint of faith] that the sufferings of the present life are not worthy to be compared with the glory that is about to be revealed to us *and* in us!"
(Romans 8:18, AMP)

Good Morning Weapon of Mass Destruction,

    I welcome you to this new day saying it was worth it! I love how the scripture text today says, "From the standpoint of faith." It helps us to understand although the suffering we are experiencing is very real, it shall NOT consume us. It has a purpose. I come to you this morning from the standpoint of Faith assuring you that your blessing is going to be greater than the pain.

    Weapon of Mass Destruction, I encourage you to begin to recite this to yourself, "My blessing shall be greater than my pain."

    From the standpoint of faith, you shall live and not die. From the standpoint of faith, greater is He in you than He that is coming up against you. From the standpoint of faith, you are already healed. You are already prosperous. You are already loved.

Weapon of Mass Destruction
"Breathe Again"

Weapon of Mass Destruction Embrace your today because it shall be better than your yesterday in Jesus name.

Lord God in Heaven, we come this morning from the standpoint of faith. Lord, we are grateful because we belong to you. We come grateful that you made us a promise, and that promise will come to pass. We are grateful that you have equipped us with the faith we need to make it through this time, victoriously. Thank You. We love you, Lord in Jesus name we pray. Amen

Tyeshia M. Thomas

Day Twenty
He Knew

"He walked away, perhaps a stone's throw, and knelt down and prayed this prayer: "Father, if you are willing, please take away this cup of horror from me. But I want your will, not mine." Then an angel from heaven appeared and strengthened him, for he was in such agony of spirit that he broke into a sweat of blood, with great drops falling to the ground as he prayed more and more earnestly."
(Luke 22:41-44, TLB)

Good Morning Weapon of Mass Destruction,

    I come to you this morning to encourage you with two words, "He Knew." The Lord knew you would have moments of despair and He prepared you for it. He left us an example about going through a rough time, but staying consistent in prayer.

    Our scripture text is talking about Jesus. This account takes place right before he is taken away by the soldiers and marched from judgement hall to judgement hall. He knew it had to happen and knowing that it was working for our good did not make it easier.
Jesus endured the ridicule, the purposed inflicted pain, the betrayal, the loneliness and so much more and He did it for you. He knew you would need to know that what you are going through is going to benefit someone else. You are going through it, but ensuring that they are

Weapon of Mass Destruction
"Breathe Again"

going to make it through it because when you could have quit, you didn't.

Weapon of Mass Destruction, I believe that an angel of the Lord is strengthening you right now. I believe you are regaining strength. I believe you are being empowered by God to keep going in the face of opposition. You will not faint because there is a nevertheless type attitude within you. You will overcome betrayal. You will overcome loneliness. You are more than a conqueror because of Jesus.

Heavenly Father the weight seems a little too much to bear at times, but we will still trust you. We trust your will. This situation does not feel good, but we will trust your will. Things do not look good right now, but we will trust your will. Our way seems a bit cloudy, but we will trust your will. Lord, there are times when we want to throw in the towel, but we will trust your will. There are times that doubt seems to creep in, but we will trust your will. Lord, we come to you to say thank you for entrusting us with such a great assignment. We love you, and our desire is to please you. We declare, "Nevertheless not our will, but yours be done in our lives in Jesus name, we pray Amen."

Tyeshia M. Thomas

Day Twenty-One
A Day of Listening

"I am listening to what the Lord God is saying; he promises peace to us, his own people, if we do not go back to our foolish ways. Surely he is ready to save those who honor him, and his saving presence will remain in our land. Love and faithfulness will meet; righteousness and peace will embrace. Human loyalty will reach up from the earth, and God's righteousness will look down from heaven. The Lord will make us prosperous, and our land will produce rich harvests. Righteousness will go before the Lord and prepare the path for him."
(Psalm 85:8-13, GNT)

Good Morning Weapon of Mass Destruction,

Today is a day of listening, but not just to anything. We are going to practice listening to the voice of God. Go back up to the top of this page, and read the passage of scripture. Then pray this prayer, listen, and write in the space provided below what you hear God saying to you.

Heavenly Father, here I am. I am in desperate need to hear your voice. I need to know what you are saying pertaining to my life. You know exactly where I am and how I feel. You know the things I refuse to uncover to others

Weapon of Mass Destruction
"Breathe Again"

and why I refuse to uncover it to them. Lord, I need you. I trust you, and I desire to be closer to you. Lord, you are my relief. You are the one that restores me. You are the only one that can cause me to recover. Lord, I don't really know how I got here. I have gone back and forth in my mind, I have repented of my wrongdoing, but I still feel nothing. My situation doesn't seem like it is changing. Help me. Speak Lord for I, your servant, your child is listening. Tell me what to do. Thank you in advance. In Jesus name, I pray Amen

    Now Weapon of Mass Destruction, listen and write. God is able. Welcome to this day of listening.

_____

_____

_____

_____

_____

_____

_____

_____

Day Twenty-Two
Yet, He still chose you

"For whatever God says to us is full of living power: it is sharper than the sharpest dagger, cutting swift and deep into our innermost thoughts and desires with all their parts, exposing us for what we really are. He knows about everyone, everywhere. Everything about us is bare and wide open to the all-seeing eyes of our living God; nothing can be hidden from him to whom we must explain all that we have done."
(Hebrews 4:12-13, TLB)

Good Morning Weapon of Mass Destruction,

    I must say God is truly blowing my mind. Our scripture text yesterday taught us how to listen to His voice. Today confirms the power of what He spoke on yesterday. It gives us a better understanding, on how much God loves us. He knows every part of us, and He still desires to use us, for His glory. He could've chosen anyone in the world, but He chose us. He chose you and me. That is great news to me!

    Weapon of Mass Destruction, God knows what happened, and He knew that it would happen. Yet, He still chose you! He still chooses to use you! He still chooses to bless you! He is still coming to your rescue. He is still defending you! He is still allowing his favor to be upon you! He is still allowing his glory to shine on you. He knew you would fail some test, pass some, and

Weapon of Mass Destruction
"Breathe Again"

He still chose you. He knew you would stumble, and he knew who would cause you to stumble.

Weapon of Mass Destruction, hold on, pace yourself, and just BREATHE AGAIN. God sees us better than we see ourselves. Remember you are who God says you are!

Let's pray

To the Most merciful Father, we know in Heaven, here we are Lord, grateful, and somewhat speechless. You know every thought, action, and reaction that goes on in our lives; yet you chose us, to carry your glory. Although, there were many times, we chose to go astray; yet, you chose to clean us up. Lord, we can never repay you for all that you do. We will never be able to truly comprehend why you chose us, but we are grateful. Thank you for loving us. Thank you for caring enough about us, to place us in one another's life to pray for each other. Lord, thank you for Jesus. Thank you for praying for us more than we think to pray for ourselves. Thank you for the Holy Spirit within us. In Jesus name, we pray, Amen

Day Twenty-Three
Today is our day of worship

"O come, let us sing unto the Lord: let us make a joyful noise to the rock of our salvation. Let us come before his presence with thanksgiving, and make a joyful noise unto him with psalms. For the Lord is a great God, and a great King above all gods. In his hand are the deep places of the earth: the strength of the hills is his also. The sea is his, and he made it: and his hands formed the dry land. O come, let us worship and bow down: let us kneel before the Lord our maker." (Psalm 95, KJV)

Good Morning Weapon of Mass Destruction,

    I woke up excited this morning. I'm excited because I'm breathing, and I know God for myself. I'm taking slow deep breaths today, and I'm thinking about who God is to me.
Our lesson today begins with O come. In other words, it is saying, "Oh come on now, we have a reason to celebrate, and it is not predicated on how we feel." It is not even about our current situation, but it is about who God is to us. As we read on further, the text describes who we are supposed to celebrate and why we are supposed to celebrate Him. I love how it keeps saying let us because it reminds me that I am never alone. That's good news to me because there are times and stages in my life when I feel alone.

    Weapon of Mass Destruction today is a day of worship. Worship is when we acknowledge

Weapon of Mass Destruction
"Breathe Again"

God for who He is and not what He's done for us. So my challenge to you today is to list who God is to you and then verbally recite what you wrote down.
Who is God to me?

_____

_____

_____

_____

_____

_____

_____

    Heavenly Father, there isn't enough lines in this book to write out everything that You are to us, but Lord, we thank You for being more than enough. Lord, we present our worship to you. You are the most intelligent and loving man that we know. You are the most creative and caring individual that we have ever encountered. Father thank you for causing us to regain strength in and through this process. You are our peace, joy, hope, strength, endurance, resilience, and so much more. You amaze us daily, and we are grateful. Thank you. In Jesus name, we pray Amen

Day Twenty-Four
God will replenish you

"Here's what will happen. While you're out among the nations where God has dispersed you and the blessings and curses come in just the way I have set them before you, and you and your children take them seriously and come back to God, your God, and obey him with your whole heart and soul according to everything that I command you today, God, your God, will restore everything you lost; he'll have compassion on you; he'll come back and pick up the pieces from all the places where you were scattered. No matter how far away you end up, God, your God, will get you out of there and bring you back to the land your ancestors once possessed. It will be yours again. He will give you a good life and make you more numerous than your ancestors."
(Deuteronomy 30:2-5, MSG)

Good Morning Weapon of Mass Destruction,

I'm excited because today is a day of replenishment. I want you to go through today expecting God to replenish you. Expect it to happen at any moment.

I need you to return all your trust to God alone. I need you to make sure that you are waiting on God to make it work this time. I need you to believe that God did not lie to you. I need you to believe that He is concerned about you

Weapon of Mass Destruction
"Breathe Again"

and your situation. I need you to know that God is willing to do it for you.

Weapon of Mass Destruction, I'm confident that God will replenish you! Now I just need you to expect God to do it today. If you are going to work today, then expect God to show you something different about your situation by the time you return home. If you are staying at home today, then expect God to show you something has changed right there. If you are going to school, then expect God to expose you to the change He promised by the time your last class is over.

Lord, we come excited and giving you thanks on today for your tender mercies. We love you so much, and we repent for not totally trusting you with all of it. Lord, we ask that you replenish us on today. We come to you like the man that said to Jesus in Mark 9:24 (KJV), "Lord, I believe; help thou mine unbelief." Thank you for showing us great mercy and releasing us from every negative emotion that has held us captive. Thank you for your speedy response in Jesus name we pray. Amen

Day Twenty-Five
A Day of Tremendous Things

"Trust the Lord and sincerely worship him; think of all the tremendous things he has done for you."
(1 Samuel 12:24, TLB)

Good Morning Weapon of Mass Destruction,

    Today is a day of reflecting on the tremendous things God has done in your life. Take a moment to think about the things only God could have done. Think of the many times you tried to bail yourself out and couldn't without God's help. Think of the times when you asked people that were incapable of helping you for help.

    Now think about how many times you doubted him. Think about how many times you messed up trying to fix it yourself. Think about how much impatience cost you and no matter what the answer was, God still performed tremendously on your behalf. I'm grateful!

    Weapon of Mass Destruction today is our day of the tremendous! I strongly urge you to set aside some time today to sincerely worship God because of the tremendous things he has done for us. Trust God to show you something tremendous today.

    Father God in the name of Jesus thank you for the many tremendous things you have done

Weapon of Mass Destruction
"Breathe Again"

in our lives. Thank you for relieving us from the tremendous pain that we have felt. Thank you for loving us tremendously. Thank you for tremendously blessing us with the healing manifestations that we needed. Thank you for blessing us with tremendous perseverance, strength, and endurance to get through every obstacle. Lord, we love you and desire to have more of you in Jesus name we pray Amen

Day Twenty-Six
Don't give up

"I have been with you wherever you have gone, and I have cut off all your enemies from before you. Now I will make your name great, like the names of the greatest men on earth."
(2 Samuel 7:9, NIV)

Good Morning Weapon of Mass Destruction,

Can I get an Amen this morning? This scripture has me wanting to scream out with praise. God is truly magnificent, and this promise right here hits home because I needed this reminder. Lately, God has been dealing with me about remembering how great He is, and has been in my life. He has been leading me to different scriptures and even allowing me to hear these same three words, **"Don't give up"** over and over again.

Weapon of Mass Destruction "Don't give up!" God has been with you on this journey. He has gone before you and cut off your enemies. He has been orchestrating your comeback. God had a plan, and his plan was for you to prosper. Yes, from the moment you entered this trying season of your life God expected you to prosper. The things God is about to do for you are going to make that pain that you have been feeling worth it. Remember, 2 Timothy 2:12 (KJV) states, "If we suffer, we shall also reign with him: if we deny him, he also will deny us:"

Weapon of Mass Destruction
"Breathe Again"

Strong and Mighty God, Creator of the heavens, earth, and all that is within them, we come to you saying, "thank you." We come presenting you our best praise, Hallelujah! Thank you for allowing us to come back from the pits and lowly places from which we have been well acquainted. Thank you for going before us and causing the things which blinded us from seeing better to be removed. Thank you for granting us peace and putting our names in the winds. Thank you for showing us that every tear we cried was worth crying. Lord thank you for allowing us the strength to have suffered for your name's sake. We love you and honor you in Jesus name we pray. Amen

Day Twenty-Seven
Welcome to your harvest season

"There is none like unto the God of Jeshurun, who rideth upon the heaven in thy help, and in his excellency on the sky. The eternal God is thy refuge, and underneath are the everlasting arms: and he shall thrust out the enemy from before thee; and shall say, Destroy them. Israel then shall dwell in safety alone: the fountain of Jacob shall be upon a land of corn and wine; also his heavens shall drop down dew."
(Deuteronomy 33:26-28, KJV)

Good Morning Weapon of Mass Destruction,

If yesterday was not enough to make you praise God, today is a better day. There is none like God. There is not one that is more faithful than the God we serve. There is no one that has the ability to love you more than God, himself. Let that thought soak in for a moment before continuing.

Can you imagine God riding upon the Heavens? This text says, "In thy help." Our help is with God and in his Excellency. I'm reminded of our promises in Psalm 91. God is our place of hiding. He is kicking our enemies of guilt, shame, defeat, fear, insignificance, poverty, brokenness, and every other enemy, out of our midst. As we humbly, hide under the shadow of God we should have great expectations that he is clearing our way to safety.

Weapon of Mass Destruction
"Breathe Again"

Weapon of Mass Destruction, you are moving into a protected place far from the enemies that have had you bound. This place will be your safe place. It will be full of unimaginable and unexpected blessings. Your season of many blessings begins now. Remember, Genesis 8:22 promises, "While the earth remaineth, seedtime and harvest, and cold and heat, and summer and winter, and day and night shall not cease."

Welcome in your Harvest!

Heavenly Father, We come praying to the God of our Harvest in Jesus name. Lord, thank You for allowing us to dwell in safety. Lord, thank You for bringing our season of suffering to an utter end. Thank You for removing the enemies that have been bothering us. Lord, thank you for showing us how to usher in the Harvest that you promised to give us. Lord, thank you for reminding us that you are in control of every season we face. Thank you for allowing us safe passage from one season to the next. Lord, we love you, and we are excitedly awaiting the manifestations of this new season. Lord, thank you for our season of Harvest in Jesus name we pray. Amen

Day Twenty-Eight
Just sit right here

"The Lord said unto my Lord, Sit thou at my right hand, until I make thine enemies thy footstool." (Psalm 110:1, KJV)

Good Morning Weapon of Mass Destruction,

Today is a sit right here type day, and I am glad about it. I hope you are ready to receive this good news, right here. God made Jesus a promise, and because we are also seated with Jesus in Heavenly places, it is being done for us too. That is great news to me! Today, I want you to keep thinking about these words, "Sit right here until God makes your enemies your footstool."

Weapon of mass destruction, I know by now you have already figured out that God is the only one that can deliver you out of the hands of the enemy of your situation. That is what makes today's lesson so relevant. God is able and willing to make our enemies our footstool. Remember, we walk by the spirit, and everything that is coming against us started in the spiritual realm. Yes, it may appear to be a person, but I don't want you to mistake this to be an individual attack. Satan is our real enemy, and he will use any, and everyone that will allow him to use them.

Weapon of Mass Destruction
"Breathe Again"

Today I want you to read this scripture, write this scripture down and then recite it aloud. I pray that as you do this that God will do what he said he would do without delay in Jesus name. I pray that you will begin to see the manifestations of this promise in your life today.

Weapon of mass destruction I love you and thank God for you. Enjoy your day!

Heavenly Father, Thank You for being wonderful. Thank You for being the one that knows what is best for us. Thank you for making our enemies our footstool. Thank you for allowing us to keep in the forefront of our minds that satan is our real enemy, and you are more powerful than him. Lord, thank you for loving us enough to see about us. Do it Lord do it. Let your will be done in Jesus name we pray. Amen

Day Twenty-Nine
Today is your day to Shout

"*Compose* a new song, and sing it to the Eternal because of the unbelievable things He has done; He has won the victory
with *the skill of* His right hand and *strength of* His holy arm. The Eternal has made it clear that He saves, and He has shown the nations that He does what is right. He has been true to His promises; *fresh in His mind* is His unfailing love
for all of Israel. Even the ends of the earth have witnessed how our God saves."
(Psalm 98:1-3, Voice)

Good Morning Weapon of Mass Destruction,

This is a day to shout for joy! Shout, because God has given you victory. Shout, because God has come to your rescue. Shout, because this is your new day. Shout, because God did it. He was able, and He moved mightily on your behalf. Shout, because he kept you fresh on His mind. Shout because his love for you never failed. Shout, because only God was able to bring you through it.

Weapon of Mass Destruction, I need you to shout like the children of Israel did after they walked around the wall of Jericho, on the 7th day because it is done. Whatever, you needed God to do is done. Take a closer look our scripture text

Weapon of Mass Destruction
"Breathe Again"

and shout for the unbelievable things He has done.

    I need you to take another look at your bank account. Have them take another look at those test results. Take another look at your situation and ask God to release the unbelievable on your behalf.

    Lord God in the name of Jesus, we come rejoicing and shouting because you are responsible for our victory. We come shouting because your love for us never fails. We come shouting because You are the only one that can make this wall standing in the way from us getting what we need fall. Lord cause everything that is hindering the unbelievable from getting to us to be removed now in Jesus name. Father cause us to receive unrestricted access to everything we need to be victorious. Lord, we thank you for doing it in Jesus name we pray. AMEN

Tyeshia M. Thomas

Over the next ten days we will reaffirm some things in our spiritual lives. Welcome to our time of reaffirmation. To reaffirm simply means to reestablish.

Weapon of Mass Destruction
It's time to Breathe Again!
It's time to remember!
It's time to reestablish!
We're long overdue for it!

"Breathe Again"

Day Thirty
Reaffirming in Christ

"Since you have accepted Christ Jesus as Lord, live in union with him. Keep your roots deep in him, build your lives on him, and become stronger in your faith, as you were taught. And be filled with thanksgiving."
(Colossians 2:6-7, GNT)

Good Morning Weapon of Mass Destruction,

I'm excited about this week because we are taking our power back and learning to breathe again. We are taking one breath at a time and rejoicing in God because the devil didn't win. We were built to last in Christ.

Today is a day of reaffirming in Christ. We are encouraged through the word of God today to keep our roots deep in him. In other words stay close to God. Stay in constant communication with him, study His word daily and keep the faith no matter what. Romans 10:17 states, "So then faith cometh by hearing, and hearing by the word of God."

Weapon of Mass Destruction, if you are not already a part of a Bible-based teaching Church; I encourage you to get connected to one. Your connections are everything. If you are already a member of a local assembly, then I encourage you to stay connected and thankful for the connection.

Heavenly Father, we come to you in the name of Jesus. Thank you for allowing our roots to be deep within you. Thank you for filling us with thanksgiving. Thank you for our week of reaffirmation, restoration, revival, and renewal. Lord, we ask that you teach us how to build our lives on you because we know that only what we do for you will last. Lord, we love you and desire to please you in greater ways than we have please you before.

Lord, we reaffirm that we will live in union with you. We reaffirm that we will do what it takes to keep our roots deep in you and we will constantly strive to be filled with thanksgiving no matter what is going on in our lives. We love, honor, respect and adore you in Jesus name we pray. Amen

Weapon of Mass Destruction
"Breathe Again"

Day Thirty-One
Reaffirming Strength in God

"Finally, build up your strength in union with the Lord and by means of his mighty power. Put on all the armor that God gives you, so that you will be able to stand up against the Devil's evil tricks. For we are not fighting against human beings but against the wicked spiritual forces in the heavenly world, the rulers, authorities, and cosmic powers of this dark age. So put on God's armor now! Then when the evil day comes, you will be able to resist the enemy's attacks; and after fighting to the end, you will still hold your ground."
(Ephesian 6:10-13, GNT)

Good Morning Weapon of Mass Destruction,

Today is our day of regaining strength. Take a deep breath and then let it out. To build up simply means to accelerate and increase. We should be increasing in strength daily by being obedient to what God is telling us to do.

Weapon of Mass Destruction, our scripture text today is a familiar passage, but a relevant application that should be applied to our everyday lives. It is time to put on the whole armor of God, and this is not a physical armor.

Our fight is always spiritual and cannot be fought with physical weapons. If you try to fight this battle in the physical realm, you will lose.

Remember, if you are in Christ you are a spiritual being. We are in this world, but not of this world. We must pray, praise, worship, bind, and loose according to the word of God. There aren't any adequate shortcuts or special methods when living for Christ. We must do whatever it takes and be obedient to the word of God because everything in this world will fail except for the word of God. Jesus stated in Matthew 24:35, "Heaven and earth shall pass away, but my words shall not pass away."

Heavenly Father, thank you for your word. Thank you for providing us with the Heavenly armor that we need to stand against the enemy. Lord, thank you for instructing us on the things that will keep us victorious over the enemy. Lord, equip us with wisdom on how to fight, when to fight and when to let you fight. Lord, we trust you. Thank you for giving us the capability to be a weapon and carry your weaponry within us, Lord, thank you for allowing us to Breathe Again, in Jesus name we pray. Amen

Day Thirty-Two
Living past your reality

"No, dear brothers, I am still not all I should be, but I am bringing all my energies to bear on this one thing: Forgetting the past and looking forward to what lies ahead, I strain to reach the end of the race and receive the prize for which God is calling us up to heaven because of what Christ Jesus did for us."
(Philippians 3:13-14, TLB)

Good Morning Weapon of Mass Destruction,

 I pray things are getting better for you day by day! I pray that you are receiving strength and comfort in your time of need. I pray that God is revealing new things to you and allowing you to see more clearly his perspective about your situation. Although pain is your reality at this moment, it must pass.

 Today our focus will be on learning to live past our reality. If it just happened, it means it is now in the past. I love our text on today because the Apostle Paul is telling us that he doesn't have it all together, but this is what he practices. Verse fourteen in this particular translation begin with I strain. This lets me know that it is not going to be easy, but it will be worth it. Getting over what has happened in our past can be very difficult because of the many emotions attached to the memory. However, it is possible. Our greatest example of suffering, and making it through is Jesus. He suffered being talked about, lied on, rejected, spit on, abandoned, denied and so much more.

> ***Weapon of mass destruction, God understands and this too shall pass. Let us carry on in truth.***

Heavenly Father, You are our truth. Thank you. Lord, teach us how to live past our reality. We desire to live a life welcoming to you. Lord, we desire for you to dwell with us. Lord, we understand that our reality is temporary, but the truth is eternal. Thank you for being eternal and everlasting. Father, we come trading in what was, could have been and what is, in Jesus name. Let your will be done. Amen

Day Thirty-Three
Reflecting on God

"Come, gaze, fix your eyes on what the Eternal can do. Amazing, He has worked desolation here on this battlefield, earth. God can stop wars anywhere in the world. He can make scrap of all weapons: snap bows, shatter spears, and burn shields. "Be still, be calm, see, and understand I am the True God. I am honored among all the nations. I am honored over all the earth." You know the Eternal, the Commander of heavenly armies, surrounds us and protects us; the True God of Jacob is our shelter, close to His heart."
(Psalm 46:8-11, Voice)

Good Morning Weapon of Mass Destruction,

    Today is going to be a great day. I just know it because God is surrounding us. He is protecting us, and nothing can happen without His permission. The better thing about that is even if He permits it to happen He is able to sustain us through it.

    Weapon of Mass Destruction, I encourage you to focus on the good things and watch God make the many wars in your life cease from having power over you. God is amazing, and He can do whatever He wants to do. So, be still, stay calm and watch God work!

Tyeshia M. Thomas

Heavenly Father, we come thanking you this morning for being the amazing God that you are to us. Lord, thank you for causing the wars in our lives to cease from having power over us. Lord, thank you for surrounding us with your love and protection. Thank you for providing us with the understanding that it takes to know that we are ok because you are in control.
Lord, we decree and declare that you are our shelter and we are close to your heart. We decree and declare that we will be still, be calm and watch you work in Jesus name we pray. Amen

Day Thirty-Four
Reclaiming Structure

"Study *and* do your best to present yourself to God approved, a workman [tested by trial] who has no reason to be ashamed, accurately handling *and* skillfully teaching the word of truth."
(2 Timothy 2:15, AMP)

Good Morning Weapon of Mass Destruction,

Today is our day of reclaiming structure in our lives. We are reclaiming our freedom. We are reclaiming our study time, our focus, our prayer time, our praise time and the time of worship that has been occupied by trial.

Weapon of Mass Destruction, rejoice because you passed the test. The trial could only last, for the time, it was allotted. It's complete, and you are free.

Now is the time to be filled afresh by the Holy Spirit. He knows more about you than you know about yourself. Open up and be filled by Him.

To the Only Wise God in Heaven thank you for granting us the courage and boldness to reclaim structure in our lives. Thank you for the wisdom to know that we needed it and the humility to be able to accept it. Lord, I decree and declare as of today I reclaim structure in my life that please you in Jesus name I pray. Amen

Day Thirty-Five
Reaffirming my verbiage

"Don't use bad language. Say only what is good and helpful to those you are talking to, and what will give them a blessing."
(Ephesians 4:29, TLB)

"Do not let unwholesome [foul, profane, worthless, vulgar] words ever come out of your mouth, but only such *speech* as is good for building up others, according to the need *and* the occasion, so that it will be a blessing to those who hear [you speak]."
(Ephesians 4:29, AMP)

Good Morning Weapon of Mass Destruction,

Today is a reminder about the importance of using our mouths to bless and not curse. Our scripture text is very blunt. The old people used to have a saying. "If you can't say anything nice then don't say nothing at all." That saying fits right in with our text.

Weapon of Mass Destruction, I encourage you to use your words wisely because your tongue has the ability to destroy and to build up. Be careful to speak those things in which you want to see and are prepared to handle.

Remember, Speak the change you want to see. Refrain and refuse from speaking negativity.

Weapon of Mass Destruction
"Breathe Again"

Father God in the name of Jesus. Thank you for blessing us with this day. Lord, teach us how to speak in a way that is pleasing to you, at all times. Lord, keep us from foolish talking, by teaching us how to guard our hearts. Lord, please keep us, from allowing the issues of our hearts to overwhelm us. Lord, we desire our speech to please you in Jesus name. Amen

Day Thirty-Six
Reevaluating your circle

"Faithful are the wounds of a friend [who corrects out of love and concern], But the kisses of an enemy are deceitful [because they serve his hidden agenda]."
(Proverbs 27:6, AMP)

Good Morning Weapon of Mass Destruction,

    Today is the day to reevaluate your inner circle because everyone can't go. Your circle has been too big, and it has caused more hardship than help. During your season of trial, there were people around you that were inwardly fighting against you. Their mission was to destroy your Godly connections. They were sent by satan to cause you to rethink relationships and connections that God ordained. Their intentions seemed good, looked good and even sounded good, but they were against your greater good.

    Weapon of Mass Destruction the enemy sent inner circle imposters, false association illusions, complaint carriers, and character assassinators to destroy us. They came well-spoken and dressed, but were sent on assignment by the devil. But, Thanks be unto God for calling forth this reevaluation. God knows best! Glory, He sees the motives and intents of every heart. Hallelujah!

Weapon of Mass Destruction
"Breathe Again"

    Heavenly Father, Thank you for calling forth a reevaluation to our inner circle of friends. Lord remove those who have run their course in our lives. Disconnect us from every false friendship. Detach us from those sent to us by the enemy with hidden agendas. Father, thank you for protecting us. Lord uncover the hidden agendas and motives of those within our inner circles. Father show us who is who in our lives. Lord, let your will be done, in Jesus name. Thank you for divine revelation in Jesus name, we pray. Amen

Day Thirty-Seven
Reaffirming your choice

"Blessed [fortunate, prosperous, and favored by God] is the man who does not walk in the counsel of the wicked [following their advice and example], Nor stand in the path of sinners,
Nor sit [down to rest] in the seat of [b]scoffers (ridiculers). But his delight is in the law of the Lord, And on His law [His precepts and teachings] he [habitually] meditates day and night. And he will be like a tree *firmly* planted [and fed] by streams of water, Which yields its fruit in its season; Its leaf does not wither;
And in whatever he does, he prospers [and comes to maturity]."
(Psalm 1:1-3, AMP)

Good Morning Weapon of Mass Destruction,

    Today is the day we reaffirm our choice to serve God and to walk in a way that pleases him. Today is the day we reaffirm our choice to faithfully study and meditate daily on the word of God. Today is the day we reaffirm our choice to monitor our inner circle. Today is the day we welcome the provision of God that will cause us to prosper.

Weapon of Mass Destruction, I encourage you to reaffirm your choice because the choice is yours.

Weapon of Mass Destruction
"Breathe Again"

Heavenly Father, Thank you for this opportunity to reaffirm our choice to serve you faithfully. Lord, we choose you. We choose your way, your will, and your agenda. Lord cause us to prosper and yield according to your word. Lord cause us to be fruitful in Jesus name we pray. Amen

Day Thirty-Eight
Reaffirming it had a purpose

"When the Lord restored the fortunes of[a] Zion,
we were like those who dreamed.[b]
Our mouths were filled with laughter,
our tongues with songs of joy.
Then it was said among the nations,
"The Lord has done great things for them."
The Lord has done great things for us,
and we are filled with joy.
Restore our fortunes,[c] Lord,
like streams in the Negev.
Those who sow with tears
will reap with songs of joy.
Those who go out weeping,
carrying seed to sow,
will return with songs of joy,
carrying sheaves with them."
(Psalm 126, NIV)

Good Morning Weapon of Mass Destruction,

Today is a day of excitement. It had a purpose. EVERYTHING we have been through had a purpose. It had to happen. The only way God could restore something is it first had to not be available.

Weapon of Mass Destruction our scripture text proves that our trial had a purpose. Its purpose had an assignment. The tears we shed produced fortunes and caused us to be restored.

Weapon of Mass Destruction
"Breathe Again"

Our tears acted as seed, was stored up in Heaven and God is sending us a return called a reward for those same tears.

Weapon of Mass Destruction, God is sending us a reason to rejoice. He is causing us to laugh again. Breathe, Weapon of Mass Destruction. Breathe Again.

Our Father which art in Heaven, You are a Mighty Provider. We could never repay you for the amount of favor you are releasing in our lives. Thank you for it. Lord, we have held on to dreams and aspirations in hope that they would come to pass. We are waiting on the day when you will allow us to see them. Thank you. Heavenly Father, we have cried more tears than we are able to give an account for, but you know. Thank you. Lord, Jesus, Thank you for praying us through and allowing us to get to the place to breathe again. Thank you for not allowing satan to sift us as wheat. Thank you for reestablishing us and reaffirming to us who we are in you. Lord, thank you for promising us more than we deserve in Jesus name we pray. Amen

Day Thirty-Nine
Reaffirming the King in my life

"Lift up your heads, O ye gates; and be ye lift up, ye everlasting doors; and the King of glory shall come in. Who is this King of glory? The Lord strong and mighty, the Lord mighty in battle. Lift up your heads, O ye gates; even lift them up, ye everlasting doors; and the King of glory shall come in. Who is this King of glory? The Lord of hosts, he is the King of glory. Selah."
(Psalm 24:7-10, KJV)

Good Morning Weapon of Mass Destruction,

Today is the day to reaffirm who the King is in your life. This scripture text today makes something within me leap every time I read it. God is a Mighty Grand God, and He is the King of Glory. He is the real King and should be the main King in our lives.

Weapon of Mass Destruction today is our day to reaffirm the one sitting on the throne of our lives. You can't answer for me, and I can't answer for you, but there are consequences for choosing to follow the wrong King.

Today I choose the King of Glory. The ONE described in our scripture text. The ONE who sent His only begotten Son, Jesus to die on the cross for my sins. Today I choose to follow Jesus and accept His blood sacrifice for me. Today, I choose to allow Jesus to come in and be the ONE who defends me. Today, I choose the Greater He that Jesus sent, to come and reside in me. Today, I choose the Holy Spirit to guide me in all truth.

Weapon of Mass Destruction, Who's your King?

King of Glory, Come Lord and have thine own way in me. Lord, clean me out and fill me with the holiness of You. Lord, I acknowledge that You are the King of Glory in my life. Come in King of Glory and cause me to exemplify You. I decree and declare that You are my King of Glory and every other king present must leave now. They are no longer welcome to reside here. I reaffirm that You are the greatness within me and ask that You reestablish Your rightful reign in my life. Thank You for being my King of Glory in Jesus name I pray Amen

Day Forty
Everything Starts and Ends with GOD

"In the beginning God created the heaven and the earth."
(Genesis 1:1, KJV)

"In the beginning [before all time] was the Word ([Christ), and the Word was with God, and the Word was God Himself. He was [continually existing] in the beginning [co-eternally] with God. All things were made *and* came into existence through Him; and without Him not even one thing was made that has come into being. In Him was life [and the power to bestow life], and the life was the Light of men. The Light shines on in the darkness, and the darkness did not understand it *or* overpower it *or* appropriate it *or* absorb it [and is unreceptive to it]."
(John 1:1-5, AMP)

"And, behold, I come quickly; and my reward is with me, to give every man according as his work shall be. I am Alpha and Omega, the beginning and the end, the first and the last."
(Revelation 22:12-13, KJV)

Weapon of Mass Destruction
"Breathe Again"

Good Morning Weapon of Mass Destruction,

Today is bittersweet because it is the end of our time together, but the beginning, of your Now. I'm excited for you. Today's scripture text may seem long, but it is necessary for you to remember. Whether we are in our Genesis or Revelation, God is still God. He was there in the beginning, and He will be with you in the end.

Weapon of Mass destruction, He is responsible for giving us life. He is the reason why we exist. He is the ONE that defends us. He is the ONE that will not leave us. He is the light that clears our darkness. He is the only ONE that knows the day, and hour that Jesus will return with our reward.

Weapon of Mass Destruction, **Breathe Again**! Jesus Died so you can breathe again. Jesus defeated death, hell, and the grave, for you to **Breathe Again**! Receive resuscitation from Heaven. **Breathe Again**. Inhale and exhale.

Heavenly Father, Thank you for divine resuscitation. We love you so very much. Lord this journey has been difficult, but thank you for not leaving us alone. Thank you for being there with us. Thank you for sending us who and what we needed at the perfect time. Lord, our gratitude towards you is greater than we know how to express. We give you a Hallelujah because it is the highest praise, but it is still not enough to show you our gratefulness in Jesus name we pray Amen

Weapon of Mass Destruction

"BREATHE AGAIN"

Welcome to your NOW!

Weapon of Mass Destruction
"Breathe Again"

ABOUT THE AUTHOR

Minister Tyeshia Thomas proclaims that her greatest accomplishment is accepting Jesus Christ as Lord and Savior of her life. She is a member of Hines Chapel A.M.E. Church in Dothan, Al.

In 2013, Minister Thomas accepted "The Call" and was licensed to preach under the leadership of Apostle Paul Horn at Hines Chapel AME Church. She currently serves as the chairperson of the Intercessory Prayer Ministry.

Minister Thomas loves serving the Lord in whatever capacity He desires. Deliverance is her testimony: She is passionate about souls being saved, and being delivered from the clutches of the enemy. By the Grace of God, and leading of the Holy Spirit, Minister Thomas shares her gift with the world. She believes in declaring daily Revelation 12:11, "And they overcame him by the blood of the Lamb, and by the word of their testimony; and they loved not their lives unto the death." Minster Thomas is unquestionably committed to the ministry of reconciliation.

Minister Thomas is married to her husband Anthony J. Thomas Sr. She's also a mother, grandmother, business owner, mentor, teacher, preacher and a self-published author who accredits it All to God. To God be ALL the glory Always!

Tyeshia M. Thomas

Minister Tyeshia Thomas is the visionary for the publishing company, A.T. Destiny Awaits Group LLC. Their mission is to inspire, motivate, encourage, and educate through books, seminars, and mentorship. They also, specialize in assisting self-publishing authors, become the best they can be.

atdestinyawaits.com

www.ingramcontent.com/pod-product-compliance
Lightning Source LLC
Chambersburg PA
CBHW070306100426
42743CB00011B/2374